Uncle Bu

Story by Joy Cowley

There are seven clocks
in Uncle Buncle's house.

There are six dogs
in Uncle Buncle's house.

There are five TVs
in Uncle Buncle's house.

There are four trains
in Uncle Buncle's house.

There are three gorillas in Uncle Buncle's house.

There are two fire engines in Uncle Buncle's house.

But there is only one
Uncle Buncle.